T0036376

TO:

FROM:

★ ★ ★

WINNING
— THE WAR FOR —
TALENT

RECRUIT, RETAIN, AND DEVELOP THE TALENT YOUR BUSINESS NEEDS TO SURVIVE AND THRIVE

CHRIS CZARNIK

IGNITE READS
spark impact in just one hour

simple truths®
▶ Small books. BIG IMPACT.

Copyright © 2018, 2020 by Chris Czarnik
Cover and internal design © 2020 by Sourcebooks
Cover design by Ploy Siripant

Sourcebooks, the colophon, and Simple Truths are registered trademarks of
Sourcebooks.

All rights reserved. No part of this book may be reproduced in any form or by
any electronic or mechanical means including information storage and retrieval
systems—except in the case of brief quotations embodied in critical articles or
reviews—without permission in writing from its publisher, Sourcebooks.

This publication is designed to provide accurate and authoritative information in
regard to the subject matter covered. It is sold with the understanding that the
publisher is not engaged in rendering legal, accounting, or other professional
service. If legal advice or other expert assistance is required, the services of a
competent professional person should be sought.—*From a Declaration of Principles
Jointly Adopted by a Committee of the American Bar Association and a Committee
of Publishers and Associations*

All brand names and product names used in this book are trademarks, registered
trademarks, or trade names of their respective holders. Sourcebooks is not
associated with any product or vendor in this book.

Photo Credits
Internal images © end sheets, Tetiana Chaban/Getty Images; page x, 10, Klaus
Vedfelt/Getty Images; page xvi, golubovy/Getty Images; page 6, YinYang/Getty
Images; page 15, 38, 96, 110, Maskot/Getty Images; page 20, Marisa9/Getty Images;
page 24, 56, 68, 76, Thomas Barwick/Getty Images; page 29, Dean Mitchell/Getty
Images; page 34, Morsa Images/Getty Images; page 44, filadendron/Getty Images;
page 51, Ezra Bailey/Getty Images; page 61, Ippei Naoi/Getty Images; page 64,
nimis69/Getty Images; page 72, Cecilie_Arcurs/Getty Images; page 78, Compassionate
Eye Foundation/James Tse/Getty Images; page 88, gradyreese/Getty Images; page
102, shapecharge/Getty Images
Internal images on pages vi, 83, 93, 107, 114, 119, 120, 122, and 124 have been
provided by Unsplash; these images are licensed under CC0 Creative Commons and
have been released by the author for use.

Published by Simple Truths, an imprint of Sourcebooks
P.O. Box 4410, Naperville, Illinois 60567-4410
(630) 961-3900
sourcebooks.com

Originally published as *Winning the War for Talent* in 2018 in the United States
by Career [RE]Search Group. This edition issued based on the paperback edition
published in 2019 in the United States by Simple Truths, an imprint of Sourcebooks.

Printed and bound in China.
OGP 10 9 8 7 6 5 4 3 2 1

No work of this magnitude is achieved alone. Thanks go out to the many people in my life who have contributed their wisdom and experience to this book:

★ ★ ★

To Dr. Susan May, president of Fox Valley Technical College, who believed in my work before anyone knew I existed.

★ ★ ★

To the best managers I have ever had in my career. You all showed me what real leadership looks like: Tim Allen, Patti Jorgensen, Bruce Weiland, Bill Guilbeault, and Roger Johnson.

★ ★ ★

To the thousands of job seekers who have trusted me with their search. Your stories are the true authors of this work.

CONTENTS

Where Did All the People Go, and When Are They Coming Back?

The shortage of workers in the United States is being treated like some type of surprise. However, anybody paying attention wouldn't be surprised.

This shortage has been a mathematical certainty for more than three decades. While there have been fluctuations in employment over that period, this "silver tsunami" was always coming. Most companies and organizations didn't plan for this changing demographic because they chose not to look. In many cases, the focus on the next quarter's profits overshadowed the looming hiring crisis that has been inevitable since the 1960s.

The math works like this.

The Baby Boomers

There are somewhere around 74.9 million people in the generation referred to as the baby boomers. This generation consists of people who were born between 1945 and 1964. Much discussion has been made about the economic impact of this generation, as their movement through every phase of life has shaped the economy of this country. Whether it was the sale of diapers (which led to the creation of disposable diapers, thank goodness), the proliferation of automobiles (in their teens), the housing boom (as new parents), the unprecedented growth of the workforce (including many women joining the workforce for the first time), and even the explosion of the motor home industry (as this giant generation headed toward more leisure activities and retirement), whole industries were born to service them.

In terms of employees, this group created an almost endless supply of labor. For the better part of the last forty years, there was no question about having people available to fill positions. "If you post the job, they will come" was the battle cry of HR managers. The trouble is that not many organizations planned on what to do when the baby boomers moved into retirement and left the market.

Generation X

The generation that came immediately following the baby boomers is referred to as Generation X. This typically refers to those born between 1965 and 1982.

For many social and economic reasons, this generation is a good deal smaller than the baby boomers. With approximately sixty-five million people in Generation X, there were ten million *fewer* people born during the

same number of years as during the baby boom. Let's just sit with that for a moment. There are ten million fewer people in Generation X than in the generation immediately preceding it. So as wonderful as it is that the labor market and number of jobs in America expanded dramatically during the baby boomer years, the sucking sound that you hear every time you post a new job today is the vacuum created by sixty-five million people trying to fill the jobs of seventy-five million people.

The Millennial Generation

The generation after Generation X is referred to as the millennials, which describes those born between 1982 and 1996. This generation is actually slightly larger than the baby boomer generation and has approximately seventy-six million people in it. While this generation has been much maligned in the media, it is actually the most tech-savvy and forward-thinking generation to date. The size of this generation can fill the shoes left open by the baby boomers in time, but they require a much different workplace than their forefathers.

The False Hope of the Great Recession

If you do the math with the overlay of these generations, you might come up with an interesting question. "Shouldn't this shortage have started to show itself a decade ago?" Why, yes. Yes, it should have.

Except for the one event that could have hidden

it from those who were actually looking—the Great Recession. The math (when these population differences should have started showing up in the labor market) says that we should have begun to see these changes sometime around 2007, sixty-two years (the normal retirement age of the oldest baby boomers) after 1945. People who study demographics were already shouting from the rooftops in the early 2000s that the shortage was coming. Until the world economy fell off a cliff.

The Great Recession artificially decreased the number of jobs needed in America at almost the exact same time the demographers were having U.S. businesses bracing for impact. The shortage never materialized. In fact, due to the massive temporary decrease in the number of jobs in America, it appeared to business leaders that this shortage was really a hoax that was never going to come to fruition. Many of them decried the warnings that were being sent out as false fear.

Between 2007 and 2012, not only wasn't there a labor shortage, there were more people looking for work than jobs needing to be filled. Each job opening was met with literally hundreds of applicants. HR managers were blessed with their choice of the best and brightest for each opening.

Someone Needs to Pay the Piper

In response to the Great Recession, a college's visionary president hired me to create a program to teach proactive job searching to displaced midcareer professionals who were affected by the economic downturn. Over the next ten years, I trained more than two thousand of these people to do a research-based job search I created called Human Search Engine. During this time, I spent every day in the middle of the battle for employment with people who had lost their family-sustaining jobs through no fault of their own. My job day and night for a decade was to help those who had lost their jobs and were now in fear of losing their houses. I became one of the nation's experts on the job search, even to the point of my process being adopted by the Employee Assistance program in Congress.

Somewhere around 2012, a funny thing happened.

The number of people coming to my classes started to go down. At one point in 2009, I had two full classes of forty desperate job seekers, each hoping for a new opportunity. By 2011, I had to cut the number of classes down to one, as there just weren't that many people looking anymore. The number of people coming to the class gradually declined over the next three years.

In 2015, I had the opportunity to become the manager of the Employment Connections department that served our college's graduates in finding employment. By the end of 2015, a shift was absolutely noticeable. No longer were we besieged by job seekers looking for work. Now almost every call I received was from an *employer* who was having trouble finding people for their jobs! The same employers who would not get back to applicants a year earlier were now literally receiving *no* applicants for their job postings.

The shortage of workers that had been predicted for so many years was finally a reality. Most employers had no idea how to react to this because they had never experienced it before. That is the purpose of this book—to bring you new ideas of how to recruit, retain, and develop talent in your organization. To show you new ways to engage potential employees and to become an employer of choice. To demonstrate that finding and retaining talent requires many of the same skills and actions that you already do in your organization to market your products and services. To give you a head start over every other employer in your area. To ensure that your organization will have all of the talent it needs to grow and thrive in the next decade and beyond.

Farmers and Hunters of Talent

If you are struggling to find enough people or the right people to staff your organization, your initial response might be to walk down to your HR area and give them a nudge. Some of the worst business managers and owners will pressure their HR staff to "do better, whatever it takes." These businesses are going to struggle for the next decade. Why? Because almost everyone in the business world has grown up in a world where finding talent was as easy as posting a job. "If you post it, they will come" has been the answer.

When that doesn't work, some managers will go immediately to offering more money to attract talent. That lever has worked for them in the past. However, when that doesn't work either, most business owners have fired every bullet in their clip and are out of ideas. This leads to additional stated or implied pressure on HR to "step it up or else." The fact is if HR knew what to do, they would have done it already. These HR people have no more idea of how to find talent than the boss who is pressuring them. What then?

Willing and Able

In every book I write, I capitalize two words every time I use them: WILLING and ABLE. The reason is that I believe that anytime someone does not achieve what you ask of them, you have to ask them and yourself if they were UNWILLING or UNABLE to accomplish the task.

▶ **UNABLE:** Lacks the physical or mental capacity to achieve the desired outcome. They want to complete the task but physically cannot without additional resources. The needed resources may be training, tools, or technical knowledge.

▶ **UNWILLING:** Physically and mentally capable of completing the task but lacks the proper motivation. Pushback or lack of understanding of the task's importance is the limiting factor.

Consider the ramifications of classifying every task that is not completed into one of these two categories. Whether it is a child not cleaning their room or a scientist not curing the common cold, this clarification simplifies every issue of this type. The way I see it, anytime someone says they *can't* do anything (including yourself), figuring out if they are UNWILLING or UNABLE to complete the task is the critical first step. The reason is that once you have this answer, you can determine how to proceed. Does the person (again, look in the mirror, my friend) lack resources or motivation?

This is critical for managers, as we often mistake UNABLE for UNWILLING and think that people are testing our authority. As my good friend and mentor once mused, "Almost never does someone do something to purposely challenge your authority. It is either that they didn't understand you, don't know how, or thought they had a better way. Your job as a manager is to find out which of these is true." Those words have stayed with me for almost thirty years.

The central question to this entire concept is this:

Are people UNWILLING or UNABLE to come to work for your organization?

● UNABLE vs. UNWILLING

After working with more than three thousand job seekers over the past fifteen years, I can say that the number one reason why your company is not receiving applications is that the people looking for jobs have no idea that you have jobs available. There are really two separate problems here.

1. The people you are trying to reach have no idea that your company exists.

If you are an HR manager or business owner, you are likely completely consumed by your organization. You spend most of your waking moments thinking about your business. That focus is exactly why you might be making the mistake of thinking that people know your business exists. The idea that people don't know that your business exists is an affront to the thousands of hours that you have spent building and growing your organization. Because *you* know it so well, *everyone* must know it that well. That is just not true. Unless you are an employer of five hundred people or more, 90 percent of the people in your geographic area have never heard of your organization, let alone what you stand for.

In my town, there are about 80,000 people. Add in the surrounding communities, and the population grows to about 250,000. I have lived in this community my entire life (fifty-five years). My work both as a job search expert and as the career services manager of the largest technical college in the area makes me one of the area's experts on what companies exist in our region.

If you gave me a pen and paper, I could write the names of about two hundred businesses in our area without using online resources. That's not too bad until you

realize that, according to Reference USA, there are 34,588 hiring organizations within thirty miles of Appleton.

Despite it being my *job* to know what's out there, I could only name about one in one hundred of the organizations in my city. If that is true for me, what do you think is true for the average job seeker? If they do not see your company name in the newspaper, in online ads, or on a hiring site, they very likely have no idea that you exist. And there is no way that they can come to work for your organization unless they know it exists.

2. People are absolutely aware of your organization, and they know everything that they need to know about working there. They are making a conscious choice *not* to come to work for you.

As opposed to never having heard of your company, the realization that some people have evaluated working at your company and have chosen to work elsewhere should scare you much, much more.

While it would be easy to be offended by people turning down a job offer from your organization, a great deal can be learned from them by asking their reason for declining your offer of employment. Without asking these questions of them, you may automatically think their decision was about the pay, or the work was too hard. But if your goal is to fill your organization with talent, then you desperately need to know why people are walking away.

If you brush off not having enough talented employees on the idea that people just don't want to work anymore, **why are other people choosing to**

go do the exact same work for your competitors?
Some people are choosing to do the exact same work under very similar circumstances; they just don't want to do it for you. Ouch!

Turning Farmers into Hunters

Examining whether people are UNWILLING or UNABLE to come to work for you is the most important thing that you can do as part of this journey. Without this knowledge, you have no idea what to change in order to change your recruiting process. The one thing that is sure is that you need to utilize the two real recruiting tools that you have at your disposal every day: your HR team and your own employees.

It would not be too much of a stretch to say that the average HR professional knows very little about finding talent in a proactive way. Posting a job ad has always been enough, and their biggest concern was how to sort through the piles of résumés that flowed

in. With the advent of LinkedIn, HR can reach out into the community to make potential employees aware of your hiring opportunities. Actively recruiting talent really comes down to getting out from behind the HR desk and becoming active in the community.

After serving as the career services manager for one of the largest technical colleges in the state of Wisconsin, I can tell you that in my experience, HR folks don't do a very good job at all in using educational facilities as recruiting centers. That never made any sense to me, as we were training and graduating students who were exactly what they were looking for. Many companies were desperately trying to find and hire welders and electricians. Not many of them chose to visit the campus to set up on-campus recruitments or hold student lunches.

In addition to trying to meet students, being part of the advisory board for one of the technical college's departments would provide almost unlimited access to instructors who were working every day with students who companies were trying to find. So why didn't they do it?

My guess is that they did not know what programs the college provided and spent zero time interacting with our career services area to find ways to get in front of our students.

Proactive recruiting at a very base level boils down to identifying the organizations that train people with your desired skill set and working endlessly to create a relationship with them. I would often shake my head as students looking for jobs would ask for help in the morning and the companies looking for those same future employees would call that afternoon.

If you want to go fishing for trout, first you must find the trout pond.

In order to be successful in implementing proactive recruiting practices for your HR organization, you need to turn HR into a sales-minded organization. Having a person come to work in your organization is a commitment for both the new employee and the company. It is someone committing their time and effort and part of their life to your organization. They have many choices for where they can go to utilize their talents, so *you* must convince them that choosing your organization is a good life decision for them. I'm guessing that sounds very different from the traditional recruiting efforts that you have done, but how have those been working for you lately?

But before we go fishing for anything, we better make sure we are using the right bait!

Going Fishing with the Wrong Bait

Most baby boomers were taught from a very young age to be driven by security. Baby boomers (as a whole) were taught that being happy in the job was secondary to being in a job that you can have for the rest of your life. The idea that you actually should be happy in your job would be laughed at by most baby boomers. It would seem like a luxury to them and something that only spoiled children would ask for. Work is pain. The only question is how much pain are you willing to put up with and for how much money? That is the equation that defined the baby boomer generation and how they interacted with their jobs, their happiness, and their money.

Start with a Different Mindset

In contrast with baby boomers, the first important thing to understand about millennials is that they are not generally motivated by security. Therefore, trying to use the values of the baby boomer generation to motivate millennial workers simply will not work, and there's the rub with most hiring practices.

Another important factor to understand is that the millennial generation was the first generation to grow up with access to the internet. They have always had the sum total of all the knowledge of the world available to them within ten or fifteen seconds simply by typing a few words into Google. Since their very first days of kindergarten, if they had a question or were looking for a different option, instantaneous content was available; that was as much a part of their day as was the baby boomer's alarm clock going off and going to a job that made their stomach churn.

This easy access to information, options, and problem-solving is something that the baby boomer generation did not grow up with. This, however, creates the tension and the problems when it comes to motivating millennials. A startling statistic is that the average millennial will change companies, *not jobs but*

companies, every three years in their lifetime. Why? Because they can. They have the ability to identify new options, different companies, different organizations, different job types, different levels, and different responsibilities almost as easily as ordering a pizza online. This creates a significant issue for the baby boomer manager trying to recruit and retain millennials.

What is interesting here is that the baby boomer manager might be frustrated by the ability of the millennial worker to have so many options and so much flexibility. Not because they think it's wrong but because there's actual jealousy—they wish they had had access to that many options during their own career. Managers from a different generation may very well see this WILLINGNESS to move from employer to employer and UNWILLINGNESS to put up with any disappointment, hardship, or frustration in a job as the actions of a spoiled generation. The odd thing, of course, is that that manager would crave that same flexibility and those same options in their own life but was raised in a different way. In order for HR managers and hiring managers to understand and really connect with millennial employees, they first have to get over their own disappointment that the flexibility and options that current workers have are ones that were never available to them. Believe it or not, this is one of the major reasons why organizations have struggled so much in connecting with and retaining millennial employees.

So what does that mean? Relating to the millennial generation starts and ends with their desire for freedom and flexibility, with much less focus on security. Everything we do to win the war for talent is going to focus on appealing to millennial workers (and even the generations after them) with the idea that freedom, flexibility, education, and growth will be cornerstones of their career regardless of where they choose to work. In order to succeed in this new normal, it is the companies that have to adjust, not the employees.

If you're a manager or owner reading this right now, what I just said might seem upside down. If you are thinking to yourself, "This is my organization. I and only I will determine what new hires get and what is available to them," you are likely going to fail over the next ten years to attract and more importantly retain the talent you need. What you as a hiring executive need to understand is that whether you like the attitude of the millennial generation or not, they are the only pool of workers available today. The rules have fundamentally changed. It's not that the employees are now getting to tell companies what they will and won't do but that there has to be a meeting in the middle where a balance between work and home life is a real consideration and not simply something that people talk about in books. Where flexibility becomes the norm. Where others lament the fact that they work for organizations that couldn't care less about anything other than producing for the company.

It is absolutely clear that if you are going to stick

to your guns and not adapt, you will be one of those losers in the war for talent. But it doesn't have to be that way.

It is time for us to embrace what the millennials already know. That in this new technology age, opportunity and possibility are everywhere. The idea of working for one company for twenty or thirty years is quaint. In fact, the new reality, the new norm, is that **we are all free agents all the time**. You work today, you get paid today, and for the most part, that is the extent of the relationship between a company and its workers.

Trying to sell security as a way to recruit, retain, and develop this new generation of workers is like going fishing with bird seed; you're done before you start.

2

Create a Sales-Minded HR Department

Imagine for a minute that your sales manager comes to you and has a very perplexed look on his face. He is clearly distraught and frustrated. You ask him what's wrong.

"Well, we have tried absolutely everything, and we can't find any new customers. I just think that nobody needs our product anymore, and we may really be in deep trouble. I know it's my job to find new customers, but it just isn't going anywhere."

You might do what any good business owner would

do and start asking questions to try to determine the cause of this problem. "What have you tried so far?" you ask.

"We have tried *everything*!" he says. "We put the best marketing minds in the company together and came up with a really great marketing piece for our products and services. We were just so sure that people would respond to it."

You ask the next logical question. "So where did you post the marketing piece?"

"Well, we found a huge internet site that gets lots of people looking at it every day, and we put it up on there. Thousands of people go to that site every day, so we just kind of waited for the phone to start ringing and the orders to start pouring in."

You are incredulous. "Did you go out and prospect for any customers face to face?"

"No."

"Did you contact our current customers to get referrals from them for new customers?"

"No."

"Did you create a profile of our existing customers and use research tools to identify other companies that might need our products and services?"

"No."

You are beyond frustrated with the shortsightedness of your sales manager. He posted an ad and just waited for customers to walk through the door? That's crazy!

Now, if you wouldn't accept that level of effort from your sales team, why are you accepting that level of effort from your HR team in looking for new employees?

The search for new employees can utilize many of the same prospecting ideas that salespeople use to find customers. But it requires proactive thinking and a WILLINGNESS to get out from behind the desk for the HR staff.

● Steps to Creating a Sales-Focused HR Group

1. Create messaging

Regardless of what product your company sells or service it provides, you have probably spent a great deal of time coming up with messaging to make it appeal to your customer. I'd like for you to begin thinking about selling your organization as a place to work in the same way.

It is helpful for you to consider some questions while creating this messaging:

- ▶ Who am I selling to?
- ▶ What is the profile of the type of person I am hoping will join our organization?
- ▶ What is their background?
- ▶ What education or experience do they have?
- ▶ What job did they hold immediately before coming to work for us?
- ▶ What are their goals for employment?
- ▶ What problem does this job solve for an employee? What advantages does this job have over its competitors?
- ▶ Are the benefits financial? Family life? Flexibility? Advancement? Prestige?
- ▶ Who am I selling against?
- ▶ Why are people choosing to go to work for my competitors instead of me?

2. Identify your target customer (employee)

No matter how good your messaging is, if you don't have a good idea of who you are trying to recruit into your organization, all that work will be wasted. No matter how good your messaging is to sell a minivan, if you put that message in front of someone looking for a sports car, they will be unmoved. Creating a profile of your next great employee is work that you need to do.

This profile will need to answer the following questions:

▶ What education does the person have?

▶ What experience does the person have?

▶ What is the life situation of this person (first job, transitional job, second career, just a job to feed the family)?

▶ What hobbies or recreational activities does this person enjoy? (Birds of a feather flock together.)

▶ Where does this person vacation?

▶ What volunteer organizations does this person join?

3. Create models for the best people in every job

It is important at this point to see that you use this type of modeling in your life every day. If you want to lose weight, you befriend people who live a healthy lifestyle to learn from them. If you want to be successful in business, you get the advice, guidance, and feedback of people who have had successful business careers. Young people very often seek the advice of people with more life experience to make sure they do not recreate the mistakes of the past.

While you will make huge generalizations inside this model, your goal is to identify people similar to your best employees and put your marketing materials in front of them. This can be done easily through a process of interviewing your best employees in each area of your organization.

The process might look something like this:

► Identify the general traits that make employees a great fit for *your* organization. This might include their abilities to communicate, show creativity, have initiative, solve problems, or be great team players or leaders. This positive profile will be used as an overarching guideline for all your hiring.

► Create categories of jobs inside your organization. This will most likely revolve around the skill set and personality type of your best people in that area of your organization.

► Interview your best people in each area to identify the answers to the profile questions you created. These people must volunteer for this interview, and you need to be clear with them about why you are gathering this information. When you explain to them that you are looking to fill their department with more people like them, they are usually quite honored to be interviewed.

4. Create career quadrants to categorize jobs

For most organizations, if we tried to create a profile for every job inside the organization, it would take us the better part of a year. Many organizations have dozens of job titles, all with differing duties and responsibilities. This would be a Herculean task that is too complex and would take too much time for most companies. The idea of assigning each job inside your organization into a career quadrant will allow you to create profiles for only four types of employees.

The first question to ask is whether the job requires working primarily with people to improve or modify their effectiveness individually or as part of a team or primarily with a process where a series of actions create a predictable result that is reliable and repeatable. The second question is whether communication is primarily in person and face-to-face, where reading social cues and adapting to the person are important, or primarily through technology, where the accuracy of information is more important than a connection with the person.

To determine which quadrant a job fits into, choose between people and process and then between interpersonal communication and technology, as shown below.

The four types of job descriptions can therefore be categorized as follows:

- ▶ Works primarily with people and communicates in person (shift supervisor or team lead)
- ▶ Works primarily with process and communicates in person (maintenance technician)
- ▶ Works primarily with people and communicates through technology (customer service person)
- ▶ Works primarily with process and communicates through technology (IT support person)

Now go through each job category in the organization and classify it under one of these four categories. After that is completed, find a great employee in each of the four categories and create the aforementioned model with them. With these four completed profiles, you now have the ability to recruit people who will naturally fit into these types of jobs.

Consider Where You're Advertising Your Opportunities and Who Is Seeing Them

Why do thousands of organizations use websites like Monster and Indeed to advertise their job openings? They are low- or no-cost options. They are widely known by job seekers. They are well known in the business community. They have quality control and even have matching systems available. They are easy and require almost no work or commitment. Seems like the perfect way to advertise your job, right?

So why isn't it working for you?

Stephen Covey was a brilliant man. He wrote several books during his lifetime, the most popular by far being *The 7 Habits of Highly Effective People*. One of the concepts that Covey spends time on in this work is the idea that you have to evaluate any proposed solution to a problem on two axes: **efficient** and **effective**.

> ▶ **EFFICIENT** means that the solution requires the least time and effort and potentially reaches the most people.
>
> ▶ **EFFECTIVE** means that the solution produces the intended and desired result.

There are not that many solutions out there for any problem where you can maximize both of these factors. Generally, you need to make a choice between varying degrees of both. A very efficient solution might not be very effective. An effective solution might not be very efficient. There are almost always trade-offs and choices to be made between the two.

Monster and Indeed are highly efficient solutions, very little work and very little cost. But why are they not bringing qualified candidates to your door?

Modeling to the Rescue!

This is where modeling comes in. As an example, if a company were to interview their best roofing technicians, what would they learn about those employees' paths? They would ask:

- ▶ What education or experience did they have?
- ▶ What job did they have immediately before coming to work for this roofing company?
- ▶ How do they spend their free time?
- ▶ What else do they use their mechanical aptitude for in their spare time?
- ▶ What hobbies do they have?
- ▶ What classes did they enjoy in high school?

With this information, you can take your marketing documents and make them speak to people who are in the same situation but are not yet in the roofing industry. You can then deploy these marketing pieces in the locations where people with the same interests might spend their time.

Let's say that in conversations with your very best roofing technicians, you discover these facts about them:

- ► Most of them took a shop or mechanical class some time during high school.
- ► They get involved in home repair for friends/family.
- ► Their favorite place to volunteer their time is Habitat for Humanity.
- ► Their free time on the weekends is often spent working on anything with an engine.
- ► They thought that regular classroom learning in a high school setting was boring, but they excelled in classes where they could use their creativity and there was a tangible result from their work.

What would you do with this information? What types of organizations would you hope to create relationships with? How would you change your interactions with your local high school or technical college? Would you be more likely to support and sponsor efforts for Habitat for Humanity?

As you can begin to see, the first step in successful recruiting is to understand who you are trying to speak to. As we create a model of this person, we can identify common traits and patterns that give us clues as to how we can effectively speak to them. It can guide us not only in *what* to say in our marketing but *where* these marketing efforts can be deployed for maximum effect.

3

Why Aren't Your Employees Recruiting for You?

It seems to make sense that the fastest, cheapest, and easiest way for you to recruit new employees into your organization would be to encourage your current employees to recruit people they know.

This type of referral solves multiple problems for an organization:

► It entails little work, cost, or time spent by HR.

► You get a referral from someone who knows this person well and can vouch for them as an employee.

► The current employee who is referring this person has a vested interest (their job!) in making sure that they only refer great people who they know will succeed.

► The current employee can explain the job and the organization to the recruit so that they know what they are getting into and come to you with their eyes open.

This is an almost ideal situation for an employer. So why aren't your current employees referring people into your organization? Chances are that they know people with the same interests and backgrounds that make them a great fit for you, so once again, we are facing **UNWILLING** and **UNABLE** as our obstacles.

UNWILLING

If your employees really are ABLE to refer people to your organization (they know there is a need, know people who might fit, and know exactly how to refer them), then you have a larger and more complex problem in your business. It can still be fixed with a dedicated plan, but before you can plan anything, there is something that you are required to do, and it might be painful: **you need to find out why people don't want to come to work for you**.

If your employees are UNWILLING to refer their friends to you, it is likely because there is something about your organization that they see as a significant negative. No matter how much money you offer them, you will never get people to lead their friends into a situation that is perceived as negative.

Every one of your competitors has employees who have similar skill sets, experience, and abilities to the ones you desire in your employees. That means there are two things that are true:

1 There are people out there who want to do the type of work that you have available.

2 Those people chose to do that work for someone else instead of doing it for you.

Fixing UNWILLING

If you think about it, if you had the best job in the best organization with the most opportunities to grow (and people knew about it), people would be lined up outside your door to apply. As I have often said, Brad Pitt and Angelina Jolie don't need to take out a billboard ad to get a date. So what is it about your organization that keeps it from being perceived as a great place to work? Let's break it down into four categories.

1. REPUTATION

Do you know what your reputation as an employer is? The best way to find out what your reputation is in the hiring community would be to talk with people who used to work for you. Make it a part of your exit interview process when employees are offboarding. Talking to people who currently work for you is not a reliable source of information. **Asking a current employee how they rate you as an employer is like asking a beauty pageant contestant if they like the way the pageant is being run.** You will likely only get answers that are candy-coated truth.

On the other hand, talking with *former* employees is a great way to get honest feedback. You may hear things that are hard to hear, but that is exactly the feedback that you need. You don't have to choose to interview employees who were disgruntled when they left. You would likely get feedback that is skewed too far negative. The best type of former employee to interview is one who moved into a different industry or moved up to a higher position with another company.

Exit interviews on the last day of employment are generally meaningless. Conduct exit interviews with valued employees thirty days after they leave your

organization to get their advice and the truth about your company. In my experience, 20 percent of people who leave want to come back but don't know how. This is their bridge back to your company.

2. PAY

Many organizations believe that the reason they are not getting new employees is that they are not the highest paying employer in their industry. This vague, overarching, and mostly false assumption keeps many organizations short staffed.

Studies say that after a certain point of income that allows an employee to create a basic life for themselves (housing, food, transportation, and some recreation), pay quickly drops as an employee's reason to accept a job or move to a new one. As a matter of fact, pay is likely either third or fourth in this list. So why do so many employers default to this explanation of why people aren't coming?

There are several reasons:

▸ It is the easiest thing to adjust and the easiest thing to blame.

▸ It is the easiest and least complicated thing to compare yourself against with other employers.

▸ If the business is not WILLING to raise its wages, then the managers can blame the shortfall on "greedy" or "unrealistic" employees who "don't understand the dynamics of business finances."

▸ It does not require any in-depth research about your organization and keeps you from the pain of discovering what is really going on.

The easiest way to solve the pay issue in my opinion is to make sure that your entry-level wage is at least on par with everyone else. Recruiting young people into your organization means that you will be talking to folks who have little work experience and may focus solely on pay to make their decision. This pay gap makes much *less* difference as people move up in the organization. Again, once a person makes enough to meet their basic needs, the rest of their needs can be filled with recognition and opportunity.

The biggest danger by far of deciding that pay is the only reason people aren't coming into your organization is that it will keep you from doing the more in-depth research that will allow employees not only to choose you but to stay with you long term.

Last note: If you truly are far behind the pay curve compared to other similar employers in your area, you *have* to have something else to sell. Whether it is flexibility, vacation, opportunity, or development opportunities, you need a flag to fly to balance the scales. If you are the lowest-paying employer in your industry and area and have nothing else that you offer your employees, the free market will keep you short staffed.

On the other hand, if they come to you for pay, they will leave you for pay. What more can you provide?

3. OPPORTUNITY

When most people start a new job, they are not really thinking about tomorrow. They are focused on today. *What effect will taking this job have on my family? Will this schedule allow me to spend time with my children? Is this the type of work I want to do and the culture that I want to do it in? What will my day look like? What is expected of me?* These are the thoughts going through a job seeker's mind at hire, so make sure you are offering a work/life balance that is appealing along with a culture that inspires.

4. FLEXIBILITY

Flexibility can take many forms. Nontraditional work schedules, job sharing, working from home, and extended unpaid leaves are tools available to you to speak to this group. Sounds like it might be time to survey some of these folks in your organization to see what types of flexibility might be of benefit to them. Of course, you still need to run your business, and not everybody gets what they want. But flexibility is often a *free* benefit that is very meaningful to this age group as well as older employees. Have you ever heard an employee complain about having *too much* flexibility in their work?

UNABLE

If your employees are truly UNABLE to refer people into your organization, then you likely have a communication gap to work through. This starts with the idea that recruiting for the organization is no longer just HR's responsibility. For years, anything having to do with hiring people was automatically funneled to the HR area. This attitude has to change in order for your organization to win.

As we communicate to the entire organization the want and the need for everyone to be part of the recruiting solution, we need to make sure every employee can answer these questions in a way that serves the organization: Are we currently hiring? What positions are we hiring for? What type of person are we looking to hire? How do I actually make a hiring referral, and how will I know how that referral works out?

These questions play out in hundreds of organizations every day. In these companies, there is often a mistaken idea that "everyone knows we are looking for people." They think this even though they do not have a focused program to explain and promote the idea of referrals into the organization. This is happening more today than ever, because even current employees may still believe that there are ten great applicants for every position you advertise, because that's the way it has been for the past twenty-five years.

Fixing UNABLE

The first step in remedying this problem is clear communication about the current needs and desires of the business. Never assume that someone working on the floor of your company knows what is going on in the minds of the people in charge of managing it.

More importantly, here is what I learned as a shift supervisor and operations manager: **the people on the floor most likely already have an answer to your problem.** These folks know exactly why people aren't coming to work for your organization. They know if it is a pay or schedule or working conditions problem. They have discussed it dozens of times on their lunch breaks and when they hang out on the weekends. They just aren't telling you.

Why? Most likely because you haven't asked.

How to Create a Self-Staffing Organization

With what we have just covered, it is easy to see why simply offering money to employees to recruit people into your organization doesn't work very well. We need to look at what truly motivates employees and discover what would be enough for the employee to take such a risk. What the money-for-referral program misses is that money is rarely enough of a motivator for employees to take this leap. Due to the transactional nature and temporary perceived benefit, the bonus program is not inspiring to employees at all. They already have some money, so more money is nice but not motivating. Two things truly motivate people to act:

1 **Recognition**

2 **Paid time away from the job**

Why do those two things move the needle for employees? Because they both create an emotional attachment to the event. Attaching emotion to an event creates memories, fond feelings that can be relived, and permanence. In my work with more than three thousand individual job seekers, I have found one thing to be universally true. Real change and learning only happen when the student attaches some *emotion* to the experience.

What this means is that if you do not create a positive emotion or memory with the referral of a candidate to your company by an existing employee, the program is doomed to failure. If you utilize the concepts of recognition and paid time away from the job and create events that generate a positive emotional response, employees will be much more likely to engage with you. Here's how you can do it using both these concepts.

Recognition

In order to motivate employees to start the process of referring potential employees, there needs to be some almost immediate recognition for doing so. In this case, the recognition does not need to be in the form of a gift or money. A much more effective way would be an award and open communication of the event to the whole organization.

Recognition for making a referral needs to be immediate and positive for the current employee. This recognition can be as simple as a thank-you card with a twenty-dollar restaurant card inside it. What if the referral doesn't work out? Who cares? How many twenty-dollar gift cards would you be willing to give out in order to get one great new employee? Sure, there will be some gift cards that don't create a great result, but the initial effect is that it gets people talking about the program and making more referrals.

It is important for you to see here that employees will not generally make referrals for the good of the company. They will make the referral if it benefits them in a way that is immediate, tangible, and creates a positive emotional experience. Implement this recognition system in any way that is consistent with your company culture. The key, however, is to make the recognition public, immediate, and positive.

Paid Time Away from the Job

First of all, I would like to encourage anyone who has employees and is reading this book to consider something about salaried employees: **for the most part,**

paid vacation is a zero-cost benefit for salaried employees.

Now, I can already hear the HR people and the finance people reading this up in arms and disagreeing with that statement. They might argue that there is a real cost to paid time off and that giving extra weeks of vacation to salaried employees drives up the overall cost of pay and benefits for the organization. They might believe that giving this extra week or two of vacation to their salaried employees is a cost without benefit. I couldn't disagree more. To prove this, let me ask a few simple questions to see if this is true in your organization.

Do you hire another person to fill that slot when your salaried employees are off on vacation? Does someone who wasn't there the day before that person went on vacation literally come into the organization? Did you pay another employee overtime to cover the duties and responsibilities of the person who is off on paid vacation? If the answers are no, then I would argue that vacation is a no-cost benefit for your employees and can be used as a benefit to attract talent instead of increasing wages.

Let's walk through this idea for a moment. What actual increased costs in pay or benefits do you incur when a salaried employee takes vacation? My guess is the answer is *zero*. The reason for this is that one of two things has a tendency to happen when someone in the office goes on vacation:

1. Another employee or employees cover a portion of the work while that person is gone.

2. The work waits until the employee returns.

Regardless of which of these two things happen, it is clear that there has been no additional cost incurred by the organization for this paid time off. Since the person is on salary, the yearly cost of that person's pay and benefits is fixed regardless of the number of days or hours that they actually work in any given year.

Now, clearly there is a limit to the number of vacation days an employee can have during the year and still be able to effectively serve the company, but what is that number? My thought is that your goal would be to get every salaried employee to the point of three or four weeks' vacation *very* early in their career with your company. This would serve as a barrier to entry for competing companies and a hard thing for your current employees to give up in order to take a job somewhere else.

Supercharging Your Referral Program

It is important to create a referral incentive program that truly motivates employees. With money all but off the board (we have discussed its shortcomings as an incentive), the most motivating incentive of all is paid time away from work. You have an opportunity here to create an incentive system that will truly have your employees talking to their friends and neighbors about coming to work for you.

This incentive program would have five main attributes:

1 The incentive is given to the employee when the person they referred is hired, not after six months or a year.

2 The paid time off is strongly encouraged to be a vacation for the entire family (or at least including the spouse or significant other).

3 The employee is encouraged to take pictures and use social media to document their time away.

4 Consent to use those pictures and social media as an advertising tool for the organization would be accompanied by some amount of money that could be used during the trip.

5. Notices about the availability of this new incentive program need to be communicated as much as possible to the employees' entire households (mass mailing to "the family of" all employees).

What we know so far in our research is that in order for incentives to work, they need to be immediate and significant, and they need to create an emotion.

Creating the Force Multiplier Effect

Once the first person refers someone into your organization successfully and takes the trip that the extra week of vacation provides, it is important to use that experience to influence other employees to do the same thing. The goal here is to have the family on their earned vacation document their trip through pictures and social media. The money you offer them to go on the trip with (say $300) would include the company's access to some of those pictures and social media posts to be used inside the organization. The employee would of course get to decide what you are allowed to use or if they want to exchange access to those pictures at all.

Once you are granted access to those pictures, it is time to use them in a multimedia display inside your organization to show other employees what they could have if they refer someone. You could even send a flyer to each employee's home to celebrate the earned vacation and show others how they could get one as well. Making the family aware of the opportunity and creating an *emotion* in their minds to associate with that referral will help you to garner support at home for the employee. You don't have enough influence over an employee to take the risk of a referral. But their spouse and family, who will enjoy the extra week of vacation, do.

Stop trying to get referrals with money. It may be an efficient way to do it, but has it been *effective* so far?

4

Change What You Are Interviewing For

I'd like to turn your attention now to the way you ultimately choose new employees through your interview process. If you are not getting the right people into your organization, there are only two possibilities:

1. The right people are not applying for the jobs.

2. You are screening out candidates who could do a great job for you in your hiring process.

If very few people are applying for your positions, then it is clear that either your message is not compelling or you are not putting it in a place where people looking for work can easily find it.

If you get lots of applicants but the people you end up hiring turn out not being great fits for your organization, then it is incumbent on you to change your résumé screening and interview process. I mean, what are the chances that you had fifty applicants for a position and *all* of them are UNABLE to do a good job for you? Maybe you are just asking the wrong questions.

Why You Hire and Why You Fire

If I am known for any one phrase across the country, it is probably this one: "People get hired for what they know but fired for who they are." Another way of saying that is we invite people into our organization by evaluating their education and experience but we most often escort them out the door for how they act and treat other people.

Long before there was LinkedIn, the only way to separate the wheat from the chaff for incoming résumés was to see if the person had a specific set of skills and experience. There was no other option.

But what if there was another way?

I'd like you to think for a moment about the best people who work for your organization, the ones you rely on, brag about, and count on every day. Is it really their technical skills that make them so valuable? The fact that they always deliver, are never late, solve problems before they get to you, are great leaders, and are loved by your customers usually has nothing to do with their technical skills, does it?

Next, I'd like you to think of the last two people you had to fire from your organization. Not lay off due to slow sales but fire for cause. What did they do that got them fired? Did those actions have anything to do with their technical skills or education? Likely not.

More than likely, they got fired because of their interactions with other people (peers or customers). Or maybe they lacked the drive to get things done on time. Or perhaps they lacked accuracy in their work just because they lacked focus or dedication to the task. When you examine the people you fire, one strange realization will likely come to you.

We hire people for what they know (experience and education), but we fire them for who they are (the way they treat other people).

Take a second to think about that. If you hire a person who does not have the exact right experience or education but is fantastic and works endlessly to get things done, how bad can it be? How much damage could they really do? How would others in your organization react to their hiring? My guess is that if they were great people, others in the organization would be more than happy to give them whatever training or help they needed to be successful.

Now imagine the other extreme. Let's say that you

hire someone who is incredibly qualified with education and experience, but they always rub people the wrong way. They gossip and create trouble. They lack responsibility.

How much *damage* can they do to your organization?

No matter how qualified someone is, their success as an employee is going to be almost solely based on how other employees and customers react to them. Even the greatest technicians will fail if they consistently anger or disappoint those around them. So why in the world don't you screen people for those abilities at least as much as you screen for technical skills? **Whoever you hire into your organization, regardless of how much education or experience they might have, is going to spend the first six months of their career being taught your company's way of doing everything.**

Now, for highly technical jobs like engineering and medical pursuits, experience is crucial. But I'm guessing that most of the people you are hiring into your organization (especially for entry-level opportunities) do not fit into those categories. Maybe an accountant fits into this category, but a salesperson certainly doesn't. Your customer service people can have literally no experience with your products and services and still be amazing at their jobs. Remember, you are going to train them to do so.

The intense focus on education and experience is only an exercise used to efficiently screen three hundred résumés into a manageable number of candidates (like thirty or so). If you want to continue to use that for the initial screening process, fine. But what in the world are you doing using it to make final decisions between two equally qualified candidates?

Once the initial screening is done, education and experience should be almost completely disregarded for the rest of the hiring process. This would require the screening person in HR to only forward to the interviewing committee those candidates who they know

could be successful in the chosen job if their information is accurate. From that moment on, education and experience should play no role in the decision-making process. If each of them is qualified for the job, then the only evaluation from this point on should be on how they fit in the organization and whether they have the drive and desire to do the job.

As an HR and hiring manager, I was always looking for five critical soft skills in a candidate:

▶ Communication

▶ Creativity

▶ Initiative

▶ Problem-solving

▶ Teamwork/Leadership

As you look at this list, I'm going to ask you to once again picture in your mind your most valued employees. Do they shine in one or two of these areas? I'm guessing the answer is yes. What we know for sure based on experience is that if an employee comes to work each day and excels at these five things, they will be wildly successful.

How to Interview for Soft Skills

Behavioral interviewing is used in many organizations across the country. The problem is that there is no way to confirm that the stories the candidate is telling are true. I'd like to think that all candidates will be honest, but the fact is that the allure of a new job can get the better of a few of them. Candidates rarely out and out lie, but they have been known to stretch the truth some. The secret to this type of interviewing is to change the questions surrounding these soft skills in a way that will not allow candidates to prepare for them.

What I have learned after doing more than one thousand interviews in my career is that surprise is the only way to get a genuine response from a candidate. The good ones prepare for what they think might be coming. Instead of asking them to tell you about a time when they did each of the soft skills well, ask them to tell you a story about when they *failed* to use that soft skill well and how they recovered from it.

Genuine people are as WILLING to talk about their failures and what they learned from them as they are their successes. It is part of the learning that makes them who they are. They are generally not ashamed of the learning; they see it as a natural way to find out what works and doesn't work. We learn almost everything in our lives through a process of trial and error. How could this be any different?

A genuine and humble person may blush a little in telling the story because they are not proud of what they did. But all any of us care about in this case is *What did you learn from it?* This allows them to tell you

how they recovered from it, which is equally important to doing it right.

In my experience, the egotistical or nongenuine person will try to talk around their mistake or even make it the other person's fault. The clever person who is trying to be someone they are not will shift the blame to someone else or try to minimize the impact of the error. These are exactly the kinds of people you want to keep *out* of your organization.

In my opinion, the main purpose of any interview is to determine three things and *only* three things:

1 Does this person really want this position?

2 Is it a good fit for both them and the organization?

3 Can you believe the words they are saying?

If you think about all the employees you have struggled with and eventually had to let go, I would challenge you to come up with one who didn't fit into one of these categories.

5

Engage and Retain Great Talent

Most organizations that are struggling with not having enough talent or employees in their organization seem entirely focused on how to bring new talent into the organization. That is, of course, necessary, but what they miss is that as they are bringing three new people in the front door because two of their existing employees are walking out the back door to go work somewhere else. It's a little bit like trying to fill a bucket with a hose and not fixing the hole in the bottom of the bucket first.

There are three main reasons why people leave organizations, and I'd like to deal with each one of them now.

The Employee Is in the Wrong Job

Putting an employee in a job that is not appropriate for their skill set or their personality is a ticking time bomb. Many of you reading this book right now have been in jobs in the past where you struggled with every day because you didn't enjoy it or it just didn't fit. An employee will put up with this for some period of time. As soon as they believe that there is no progression and that this job (the job that is so difficult and frustrating for them) is their job for the long term, they will almost immediately start looking for another place to work. There is perhaps nothing more frustrating to an employee then doing a poor job even though they are doing the very best they can. In other words, a main reason why people leave organizations is that companies put square pegs in round holes.

The loss of an existing employee because they are in a job not appropriate for their skills, abilities, or personality type is very expensive. Most studies suggest that the cost of replacing an employee in an organization is 30 percent of their annual salary. That means that replacing a $50,000 employee is approximately $15,000 in time, effort, training, and lost productivity. I say this very specifically for those managers who do not want to spend money on training for engaging their employees. If you assigned a cost to every employee who left your organization, you would see that any money spent on training and engagement pays for itself very quickly. Unfortunately, most organizations are only focused on cost on the front end, and once they have the employee in place, they no longer track or even consider the cost of that employee leaving. That was mostly the case because there were always other employees who could be hired. That is no longer true today.

It is very rare that any employee purposely does a poor job. That means that an employee who is doing a substandard job anywhere in the organization is most likely a victim of poor training or of being in a job they never should have been in in the first place. The main cause of this square peg in a round hole problem is hiring just anyone under time constraints to fill the spot. There's an old saying that I have become incredibly fond of in the hiring process:

If you need it bad, you'll get it bad.

The Solution for When the Employee Is in the Wrong Job

The interesting thing here is that if you would like to make this happen inside your organization, you can make it happen for exactly zero dollars. That's correct. You can implement a strategy to increase the effectiveness and appropriateness of every hire for no cost other than a little bit of time. How can you do that? The answer is in the website 16personalities.com. This

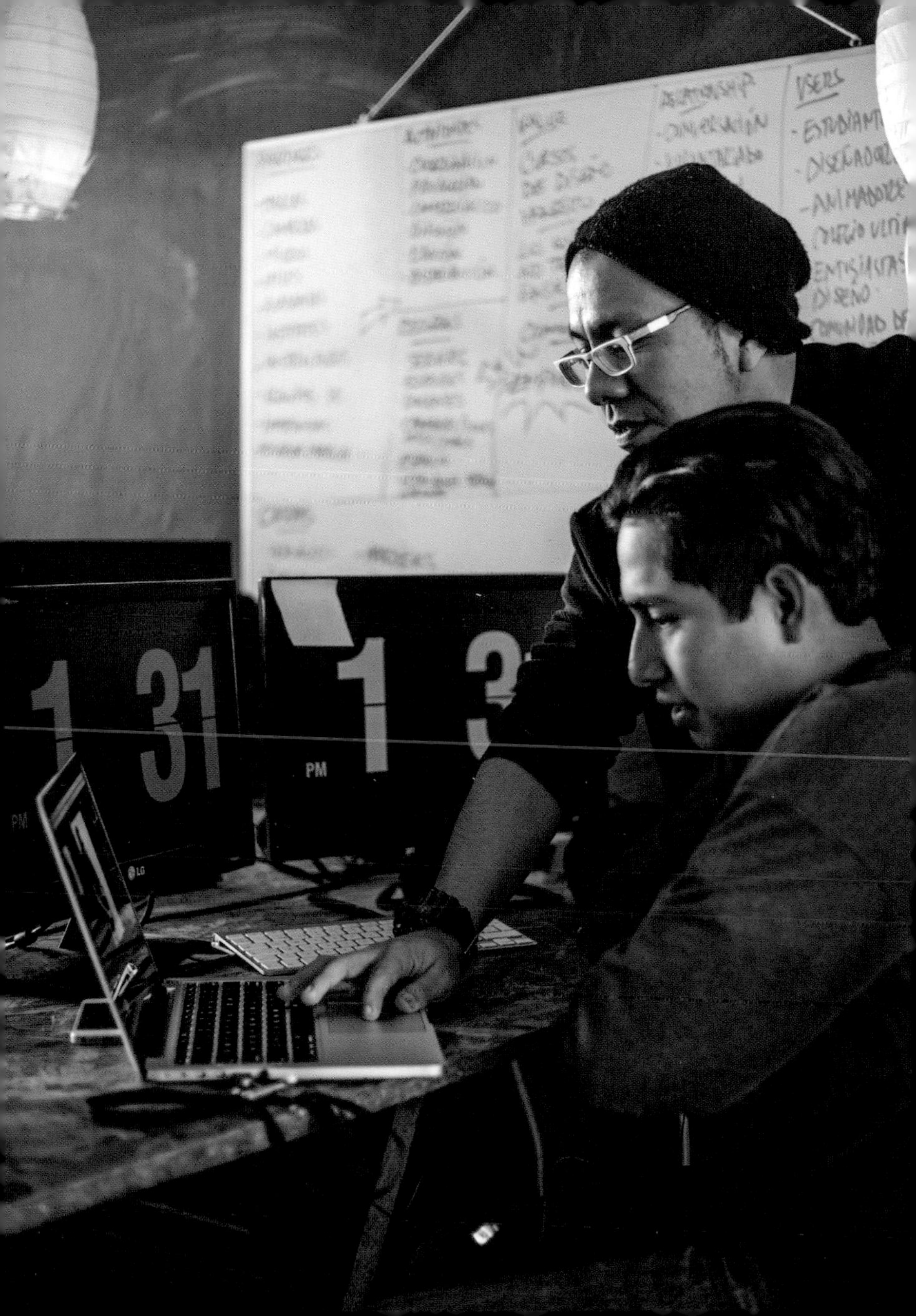
USERS
1 31
PM
LG

website contains a free personality test and results for every personality type once it is determined. Included in that is a list of jobs that are appropriate for each of the sixteen different personality types. While the exact job a candidate is interviewing for might not be on that list, jobs with similar duties and responsibilities could be a great fit.

Negative Interactions

Study after study suggests that the number one reason people leave a job is negative interactions with their direct manager or supervisor. In fact, this is so prevalent that I will spend time here talking not about how to change your employees but how to change your managers and supervisors into people your employees really want to work for.

The solution is relatively straightforward, but it comes in two different forms. As I talked about in the paragraph above, personality profiling is a great way to determine whether somebody can be an effective leader. The mistake that many organizations make is that they take the most senior person in any technical skill and make them the manager. Then somehow the organization is surprised that this person (who was an amazing technical person) ends up being really bad with people, and they get complaints about that technical person's leadership style.

It's as if you found the most reliable car in the world and then decided to use it to cross the ocean.

This manner of promoting people goes on in the vast majority of organizations. The assumption, of course, is that if somebody is good at the work, then they will be good teaching other people to do the work. While that would make somebody an outstanding technical trainer, it is not an indicator of how well they will be able to lead and train people and turn them into an effective team.

Think about the best managers you've ever had. Do you remember them as being the most technically capable people in the organization? Not likely. More likely is that those people were compassionate, good listeners, and fair, and they had the ability to motivate people to work effectively in a team.

The Solution for Negative Interactions

If your organization is not actively putting your managers and supervisors through leadership training, consider starting that *immediately*. There are dozens of programs out there, and many of them are very good. For any you select, ensure to include active listening skills. Organizations value people who can speak well but far less often note if their leaders listen well. Many of the most highly paid people in your organization are likely in those roles because they can inspire people, help customers in a time of need, or close the sale. As a society, we value extroverted speakers as they symbolize strength, confidence, and intelligence. At least that's what we think. The problem is that most managers who are struggling with their employees are first and foremost struggling with listening. Here's a question for both that speaks to this:

"When was the last time that an argument you had was not a misunderstanding?"

Active listening is teaching people that listening is much more than simply waiting to talk. Active listening is all about not only hearing the words but understanding the *intent* of the person you're listening to. This is most easily achieved by repeating back to the person speaking to you a summary of what they just said *and* what you believe their intentions were. It's not just a misunderstanding of words that gets people in trouble, it's a misunderstanding of the *intentions* behind those words.

If you begin to model active listening at the highest levels of the organization, it will quickly filter down to every other level. Taking time out of the workday to actively teach this to your employees is an indication to them that they are really important and that any misunderstanding between them and their

manager can be managed and fixed. Perhaps most importantly, it is up to your managers and supervisors to understand that it is their responsibility to initiate fixing problems of misunderstanding. Only they have the authority to take the actions that will remove the fear and anger from most manager/employee relationships. Most employees will stay silent for months and perhaps even years before they approach their manager with the issue. So it is up to the supervisor or the manager to identify indicators in a person's work that may be one of the first signs of frustration in the relationship.

Everybody Wants to Build Their Own Path

The third reason employees leave is that they lack vision for how they will develop in the organization, and they lack understanding about what control they have over their future. This happens more often than you would think, even to employees who have been with the team for five, ten, fifteen or more years. Most organizations spend a great deal of time on the front end of hiring people, making sure they get the very best people they can. They take time to train the person and make sure initially that they are doing a really good job and are happy. But after several years, it is common for an employee to become frustrated and even disgruntled with the lack of development inside the organization. This frustration is a growing seed of angst that eventually blossoms into looking for a new job. The problem is this frustration normally goes unnoticed or unseen by the employee's direct manager until the day that employee gives their notice. And when that happens, it is very common for the manager to say to that employee, "Why didn't you tell me you were unhappy?"

The better question is: **Why wasn't there a plan in place for the employee to guide their own career and keep themselves satisfied and challenged?**

At a base level, it seems ridiculous to me that anyone should have their development in the hands of someone else. The only reasonable expectation is that employees be given the opportunity and the tools to be in charge of their own careers and their own development.

Do you remember your last conversation about a development plan for you? My guess is there were some vague generalities discussed around communication or cross-training or increased responsibilities within the organization. It all sounded great to you. The problem was there was nothing concrete to execute that plan. In fact, your manager was responsible for your career path in terms of showing you opportunities to grow personally and professionally. I don't know about you, but the only person I want responsible for my future is me. But is that really possible?

Most employees would gladly take responsibility for their own development inside their organization if they were given the chance. More importantly, the feeling of being in control of their own future is the glue that will make employees want to create five- or ten- or even twenty-year careers with a single organization. If you are reading this, my guess is this seems pretty attractive but out of reach.

The promise here goes far beyond getting employees to stay in your organization and saving the cost of turnover. The real opportunity afforded by implementing development planning (driven by the employees themselves) is to create succession planning that can be guided, monitored, encouraged, and measured. The equation here is relatively simple. The employees want control over their careers. The management of an organization wants to develop the next generation of leaders. Why not give employees the tools and the systems to conduct their own internal career mapping as a research project that they are responsible for?

The Solution for Employees Wanting to Build Their Own Path

While most employees currently have to rely on hope for their next promotion, your employees can set their own course, do their own research, prove to the organization that the job they have targeted is a great fit, and conduct all the internal research to confirm their hypothesis.

The benefit of this type of program that you may

not have thought of or considered is its ability to create employee-initiated cross-functional and cross-departmental conversations inside your organization. This can lead to increased communication and decreased confusion and misunderstanding. My guess is that if you could encourage these types of conversations within your organization, that would be a pretty positive thing for you. The beauty here is that these conversations are a natural end result of the internal career mapping conversations that employees will be having every day. So how exactly does internal career mapping work?

What do employees lack currently that keeps them from being able to identify future opportunities inside your organization?

My guess is it boils down to three things:

1. Knowledge of what their personality type and transferable skill sets are and what problems they solve

2 A systematic way to sort through positions in the organization that are a next logical fit based on their education, experience, and desired career path

3 Access to information about those positions from people who have or have had those jobs in the past

All you require as an organization to encourage and empower employees to create their own internal career map is to make them ABLE to perform that research project inside their current role.

6

From What to Why: Creating SMEs

In every new role that I've had in my life, regardless of whether it was in a large organization, a startup, or an educational or public service role, my training focused on *what* I should do. Training centered around tasks, outcomes, timelines, and measurements. Especially before I was in leadership roles, the training for my jobs could best be described as "how to pull the plow." Very little time or attention was paid to any history or significance of the role or how it affected anyone else in the organization.

If you start to think about training people to move into entry-level leadership roles, you will note that much of their training focuses on *why* they are doing something. The fact is that most supervisor and manager roles differentiate themselves from the roles of individual contributors because the work they do and the guidance they give affects other people. Whether those other people are internal or external customers makes little difference. Understanding the *why* of doing something is a critical component of training new leaders. It helps them develop problem-solving and critical decision-making skills. It allows them to explain their decisions to others. It allows them to understand the ramifications of their actions and decisions.

One very positive way to start down this path is to **encourage** all employees to ask *why* they are being asked to do something. When they understand *why*, they grow. When they understand *why*, they ask great questions that keep us from making mistakes. When they understand *why*, they come up with new ideas that save time and money. When they understand *why*, they share what they have learned. When they understand *why*, they feel like part of the answer...not just a cog in the wheel.

Why, at *all* levels of the organization, equals growth. When people are challenged to grow in a positive way, they tend to stay. When people stop learning and growing, they start leaving.

Creating SMEs

The idea of developing employees in your organization may sound intimidating, but it doesn't have to be. First, the amount of training that most new managers or supervisors get on creating development plans for their employees is negligible in most of the organizations. Even the best managed organizations that take the time and effort to really train and educate new leaders focus mostly on the nuts and bolts of running their new department or team. The blocking and tackling that needs to be managed for the department carries with it a great deal of documentation and history. Examples of the right way to find answers, communicate information, and report on results are usually plentiful. But what training do these new leaders get in creating development plans for their new reports?

Secondly, I have always thought that coming up with a development plan for anyone other than yourself is a tough task. Without knowing a person's personal and professional goals, home situation, interests, previous training, areas of weakness, personality type, and natural skills, how could *anyone* effectively create a development plan for another human being?

Lastly, depending on the organization, the available time and assets needed to carry out development plans often shrink when time is tight. Development often takes a back seat to virtually every other immediate need of the organization. Managers do what they are rewarded for doing. When was the last time your managers got a bonus for implementing an effective development plan? While noble in its intent, the traditional development process is arduous and hard to manage.

But what if there was another way?

What if there was a way that every employee in your organization created their *own* development plan? What if each employee was given the opportunity to create expertise in areas that would serve the organization in very real ways for years to come? What if we could judge the initiative and desire to grow of each employee without ever having to lift a finger?

The Value of Subject Matter Experts

For many years, education and technical businesses have created Subject Matter Experts (SMEs) within their organizations. What is a SME? It is an employee who does self-study to become deeply knowledgeable on any topic. It is a person who chooses one topic to become an absolute authority on.

Think about your organization as it exists today. You may already have some unofficial SMEs who you consistently rely on—they could be someone who has been running a certain machine for twenty years, someone who knows the tax code inside and out, someone who understands how to price new products, or someone who has a deep level of technical knowledge on a raw or finished material that you produce. These are the people who put out the fires when things go wrong, or the people whose opinion you rely on without a second thought. Unofficial SMEs have gained their knowledge without formal request. They do so because that topic is personally and professionally important to them.

The idea that I am putting forward is that you can create a **formal, official SME program** in your organization. I would start by getting a group together and identifying topics that are critical to the success of the company. The topics could be technical or topics for which you have brought in a consultant for in the past. What is a consultant other than an SME who you contract? Creating a list of technical topics for SMEs in your organization is as easy as looking back over the crises that happen over and over and require outside help to fix.

There are some universal topics that all organizations would benefit from having SMEs on. These include:

1. **Analytical problem-solving:** We all think we are good problem-solvers, but some of us are true *pros*. A SME on analytical problem-solving could be brought in to help with any project or initiative that has been bogged down.

2. **Active listening:** Active listening not only clarifies communication but teaches people to lead with the intent of the message.

3. **Group facilitation:** If you have endless meetings with little getting done, it is entirely possible that

the time spent in meetings is not effective. There are volumes of information on best practices to reduce meeting time while increasing their effectiveness.

4 **Lean manufacturing principles:** These time- and money-saving principles have been used for decades by manufacturing organizations (including Toyota), but their application in *all* types of organizations has literally transformed companies.

5 **Conflict resolution:** This skill is the ability to find root causes of disagreements and move toward win-win resolutions.

With a little research, you could find dozens more topics that fit these criteria. Along with all of the technical topics that are particular to your industry or organization, it would be easy to have twenty to thirty topics to have SMEs on. So how do you make this happen?

1. Identify all the topics that you desire to have SMEs on.

2. Identify employees who have earned the opportunity to develop in the organization based on outstanding work and attitude.

3. Starting in their third year of whatever job they are in (or when you believe they are ready for more responsibility), ask those employees if they want to participate in this program. Present them with a list of the topics that you want to create SMEs for and have them choose one based on existing experience on the topic.

4. Allow them two to four hours per week to study this topic using all the free online resources available. Google and YouTube used in combination is an amazing resource of information.

5 After no fewer than six months of study, they are to prove their SME status by teaching everything they know about the topic to you or their direct supervisor. The supervisor should have enough knowledge on the topic to ask questions and challenge them in a positive way.

6 After the manager is satisfied, they can arrange for the new SME to hold weekly or monthly department meetings where they give an overview of the topic and teach the topic basics to everyone in the organization.

7 Once this training is done, the manager can give some reward to the SME, such as a bonus or bump in hourly wage. Implement whatever reward the organization decides is appropriate and motivating.

What Are the Advantages of Creating a SME Culture?

The first and most obvious advantage is that, while people in your organization want to climb the corporate ladder, there are only so many supervisor, manager, or department head jobs that exist. You can't create a new layer of management just to give people a place to move. SME training creates an unofficial new job category and level that rewards driven people without creating a cost burden.

Secondly, people are in charge of their own learning and development, and they are doing it on a topic that they already have interest in. They may likely do some of their learning outside of work, which is their own choice and *not* to be expected by the company.

Perhaps most importantly, the knowledge that the SMEs gain can be taught to the whole organization with little commitment of time or money. The SMEs learn presentation and teaching skills that are critical to new supervisors and managers. It is said that "a rising tide boosts all ships"—this is most certainly true in this concept.

Developing the Next Generation of Leaders

The following process to develop leaders has been proven effective with more than three thousand mid-career professionals. More important is the realization that the process that I'm about to discuss has been used by companies to develop and sell *every* type of product *ever* sold. This process has not only been proven over the last fifteen years of my training courses, but influences you every single day of your own life to get you to purchase items both large and small. This is not a theory. In fact, this is very likely the way your marketing department has chosen to sell your products or services to your customers. I trust that you will find these three basic steps familiar.

Definition Phase

In the definition phase, the employee learns everything they possibly can about their own personality type through online research. This will help them better understand their values, how they make their decisions, and what is truly important to them.

The next step is for your employees to write out five of their most significant work-related achievements. They should write them out in paragraph form. The purpose of this exercise is to not only identify when the employee was doing the correct work in the correct situation but to identify their natural skill sets.

Now take a look at each of those achievements. Identify which skills were most commonly associated with them. In this case, each employee will identify the skills that they are most comfortable with, enjoy doing, and, as importantly, have used to create an outstanding end result.

The last step in the definition process is for the employee to create a hypothesis based on what they have learned from their achievements and skills about the type of work, the types of responsibilities, and the types of problems they hope to solve in their next position. This hypothesis might sound something like this: "I am looking for a position involving monitoring safety, quality, and productivity for a manufacturing department focused on continuous improvement and lean manufacturing ideas."

The reason this step is so important is that it is very common for an employee to simply say "I'm looking for a job with more responsibility or in a different department." With this type of vague generality, it is impossible for them to identify actual positions that exist inside an organization that they would like

to focus their research on. The ability to clearly define the tasks, duties, responsibilities, level, and deliverables that they hope for in their next position is a critical piece for them to be able to examine all positions that exist inside their organization and find those that fit.

Research Phase

The research phase in internal career mapping begins with using the skills the employee identified during their definition phase. The goal here is to use those skills and those terms to search through a list of job titles and job descriptions inside the organization, using a keyword search, so that only jobs that fit those criteria are shown as possibilities to the employee. That may not seem like a difficult task if your organization only has ten different job descriptions. But consider an organization that has more than twenty thousand employees, more than fifty different locations, and almost one hundred different job descriptions. The number one reason that employees do not currently drive their own development inside an organization is because they just don't know what possibilities exist.

Another part of the research phase of the process involves the employee not only identifying a position that they believe is a natural fit for them going forward but the need for them to justify their decision and prove their hypothesis with facts and evidence to their own manager or somebody in the HR area. To be clear, this process has nothing to do with people getting whatever they want inside an organization. That's just madness.

It is only after the employee's hypothesis is confirmed with somebody in authority that the employee is given the go-ahead to conduct the last phase of this research project.

● Confirmation Phase

The long and short of confirmation is that up until this point, everything the employee knows or thinks they know about this position is conjecture. It is based on what the employee thinks they know about what it takes to be successful in this next job. Confirmation is exactly what it sounds like: confirming by talking with people who do or have done the job that this position is what they thought it was and that they still want to continue their development path toward filling that role.

There is little worse in an organization than having the wrong person in a role. In the confirmation phase, the employee will conduct informational interviews with people inside the organization who have direct knowledge of the duties, responsibilities, and requirements to be successful in the targeted role. There is no replacement for learning about a role by talking to people who have been in the trenches and successfully executed the role's requirements.

As with the other parts of the process, the confirmation phase runs through the employee's manager or a trained coach. During the employee's conversation with their manager, they will ask for advice as to which people inside the organization the manager believes would be helpful to talk with about this position. The manager and the employee will again confirm the goals and the reasons why this particular position has been set as a future goal. This additional conversation between the manager and the employee can do nothing but strengthen that relationship.

After the manager suggests a person inside the organization for the employee to talk with, the employee sets up a conversation with that person who has experience that they can learn from. They can get that person's view on the role and the appropriateness of the role for the employee going forward. The employee will ask for that person's advice, guidance, and feedback as it applies to their research project regarding this potential future opportunity.

The employee will learn all the pluses and minuses, responsibilities, and deliverables of the role. Through these conversations, the employee will make a final determination about whether this role is a great fit for them going forward. They then set this role as their new target development opportunity.

Gap Analysis: The Final Piece in Employee-Driven Development

With all the research completed, the last part of internal career mapping has to do with creating and executing what I refer to as a gap analysis. It is the closing of these gaps to make the employee fully qualified for the target position that is the real payoff for this process.

In order for an employee to be fully qualified for the position they have targeted as their next internal opportunity, there are very likely going to be both educational and experience gaps that exist. With their manager or their internal coach, the employee identifies what experiences and what education they would need to be a serious candidate for this position the next time it becomes available. With this knowledge, the employee can execute a self-determined plan to not only develop themselves and their skills but be a serious candidate for higher-level positions inside the organization in the future.

With this idea in mind, I would suggest that the reason most employees do not develop inside an organization is not because they are UNWILLING but because they are currently UNABLE. They lack a clear executable process in order to drive their future success in the organization. There is nothing more motivating in the world for any employee than self-interest. A company's future success relies on its ability not to plan an employee's future for them but to give them the tools to create that pathway for themselves.

This is the promise of winning the war for talent. No program of the week, no fairy dust, and no quick fix. You will win the war simply because you will find, engage, and develop the best talent possible. Isn't that all anybody is looking for?

· ABOUT THE AUTHOR ·

 **CHRIS CZARNIK** has spent twenty years analyzing hiring from every angle. He has served in HR, hiring manager, and operations manager roles for Fortune 500 companies for more than a decade. Chris knows the joys and frustrations of trying to find people who truly fit an organization's culture and values.

From the other side of the desk, he has provided outplacement services to more than two thousand mid-career professionals. This experience has given him a perspective few have. Chris not only understands what employers are looking for but also why people come to and leave organizations and what they are truly looking for from their next employer.

In 2013, he created the Human Search Engine process that serves job seekers. This process is used by colleges and organizations across the country, including in the U.S. Congress. Internal career mapping was the next logical step after all the work he has done inside organizations over the past decade.

Chris owns Career [RE]Search Group. He creates digital and print products to help people find the right roles in the right organizations and help organizations find the right talent for their culture.

Resources

You can learn more about us, our company, and our products (or follow our blog) at:

chrisczarnik.com

And connect with us at:

linkedin.com/in/chrisczarnik/

NEW! Only from Simple Truths®

IGNITE READS
spark impact in just one hour

IGNITE READS IS A NEW SERIES OF 1-HOUR READS WRITTEN BY WORLD-RENOWNED EXPERTS!

These captivating books will help you become the best version of yourself, allowing for new opportunities in your personal and professional life. Accelerate your career and expand your knowledge with these powerful books written on today's hottest ideas.

TRENDING BUSINESS AND PERSONAL GROWTH TOPICS

 Read in an hour or less

 Leading experts and authors

 Bold design and captivating content

EXCLUSIVELY AVAILABLE ON SIMPLETRUTHS.COM

Need a training framework?
Engage your team with discussion guides and PowerPoints for training events or meetings.

Want your own branded editions?
Express gratitude, appreciation, and instill positive perceptions to staff or clients by adding your organization's logo to your edition of the book.

Add a supplemental visual experience
to any meeting, training, or event.

Contact us for special corporate discounts!
(800) 900-3427 x247 or simpletruths@sourcebooks.com

LOVED WHAT YOU READ AND WANT MORE?

Sign up today and be the FIRST to receive advance copies of Simple Truths® NEW releases written and signed by expert authors. Enjoy a complete package of supplemental materials that can help you host or lead a successful event. This high-value program will uplift you to be the best version of yourself!

— SIMPLE TRUTHS —
ELITE CLUB
ONE MONTH. ONE BOOK. ONE HOUR.

Your monthly dose of motivation, inspiration, and personal growth.